The Duke of Northumberland

When my wife and I moved to Alnwick Castle in the mid 1990s, we recognised that we were just a link in a chain of Percy custodians that stretched back nearly 700 years and that it was our job to ensure that chain continued. Since then, much of the interior has been restored along with many of the great works of art and furniture; significant parts of the crumbling outer walls have been repaired or replaced and the Castle is in pretty good condition. The Alnwick Garden has added a new dimension, filling a gap that had been missing for generations and reflecting the passion of the present Duchess to create a garden with global appeal that would amuse, stimulate and educate the visitor. Alnwick Castle has hosted many famous films including Harry Potter and Elizabeth but it is much more than a film set. Built as an austere border fortress, it was virtually a ruin by the eighteenth century and then transformed with the sumptuous interiors that the visitor now experiences, filled with wonderful treasures collected by the family over many generations. It is as an important part of our national heritage but it is not a museum run by committee; it is a family home, where children play and pets chew the carpet, where the individual idiosyncrasies of owners, past and present, are reflected in the art, furniture and decoration. Visitors are very important to us, helping to pay for the maintenance and restoration of our heritage. But we are well aware that the 'visitor experience' needs to excite, amuse, educate and satisfy a wide range of people of different ages and interests at a reasonable cost. We will continue to try and improve the experience and hope you will return every now and then to see how we are getting on.

Northumberland

ALNWICK CASTLE
Home of the Duke of Northumberland

CONTENTS

Changes may be made within the rooms and to items on display.
Restricted opening times may apply to particularly light-sensitive rooms, such as the Chapel.
Photography is not permitted within the State Rooms.

The CASTLE SITE

The story of Alnwick Castle emerges in the Norman age. At that time many motte and bailey castles appeared in the old Saxon earldom of Northumbria. Layout of the site still carries characteristic features: defensive development on a natural bluff above a river, a defensive bailey within the line of an outer ditch and the creation of an impregnable motte within the line of an inner ditch. Today, these form the outer bailey, inner bailey and keep of the castle.

Next was the building of a 'shell-keep' in stone which developed as a series of semi-circular towers linked by curtain walls around an inner courtyard. The Norman chevron design decorating the archway of the keep's gatehouse (pictured right) is of the first part of the 12th century; so too are the small regularly shaped square stones to be found in stretches of the curtain walls (north side outer bailey; east side inner bailey).

NORMAN CHEVRON DECORATION OF THE GATEWAY TO THE KEEP

LOOKING WEST ACROSS THE INNER BAILEY TOWARDS THE KEEP; TO THE RIGHT, THE POSTERN TOWER, CONSTABLE'S TOWER AND HOTSPUR'S SEAT

A chronicler described the castle as being 'most heavily fortified' in 1138. The builder of this fortress was the Norman magnate Eustace FitzJohn who had grown powerful in the service of King Henry I and through marriage to the heiress of Yves de Vescy. Eustace's descendants adopted the Vescy surname. The great Alnwick barony, of which the castle was head, provided the crown with a dozen knights.

GATEWAY TO THE ALNWICK GARDEN

At this time Alnwick lay within the overlap of the feudal powers of the English and Scottish kings. In the 12th century it came into the English orbit and this threatened the political independence of the Vescys. Hostility between the magnate Eustace de Vescy and King John, who visited Alnwick on his tour of his northern borders, stemmed from royal encroachment of power.

POSTERN TOWER, WATERCOLOUR BY D. MOSSMAN, C. 1860

 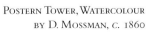

Details of the castle site as seen today emerged in the first half of the 14th century, shortly after the castle's acquisition by the first Percy lord of Alnwick in 1309. The outer bailey was equipped with a series of strong towers, the largest being the Abbot's Tower at the exposed north-western angle. These towers were interspersed at intervals by the smaller guerites or watch-towers built on the heads of curtain walls.

THOMAS TRESWELL'S PLAN OF ALNWICK CASTLE
IN THE EARLY 17TH CENTURY

The middle gateway was also built then. The 14th century pattern of defences in the inner bailey was similar to those of the outer bailey: the curtain wall is punctuated with towers and guerites. The Postern Tower provided another exit from the castle. Sorties could be made through the Postern gate to prevent attempts by besiegers to mine under the wall of the keep on its exposed north flank. The final Percy embellishment of this recently acquired fortress was the addition of semi-circular towers to the shell-keep and the building of the pair of octagonal towers onto the keep's gatehouse. The heraldic shields of arms decorating the tops of the gatehouse towers link their building to the second Percy lord.

The building of the barbican, Alnwick's most distinctive military feature, complete with ditch, counterpoised drawbridge and outer tower and gate, may have been a later 15th century structure. It was intended to strengthen the castle's gatehouse and walls, shown to be vulnerable as a consequence of numerous sieges in the 1460's. It was modified in 1475 when the 'fetterlock' badge of the Fourth Earl was put in place above its outer gateway.

Additional buildings and structures, since gone, are described in written and pictorial sources. Thomas Treswell's plan of the early 17th century shows ranges of stable buildings and an exchequer house next to the gatehouse in the outer bailey as well as a chapel, pant and additional tower standing in the inner bailey. Peter Hartover's late 17th century painting (see p.45) shows the chapel in ruins and provides a good elevation of the exchequer house. Written evidence as early as 1314 lists the strength of the garrison: 3 knights, 38 fully armed soldiers and no fewer than 40 'hoblars', mounted troopers, who formed the backbone of the military force on the borders with Scotland.

THE OCTAGONAL TOWERS AT
THE ENTRANCE TO THE KEEP

A survey of 1538 reveals the daily routine of the castle's garrison who had within the castle walls a bakehouse, brewhouse, military storehouse, cart sheds and stabling for 160 horses. A blacksmith's shop was conveniently situated immediately outside the barbican. The straight stretch of highway from the barbican through Bailiffgate and Ratten Row provided the garrison horses with an exercise ground. In 1538 the castle needed a new drawbridge, 'an iron yett' or gate for the gatehouse, the replacement of roofing leads and gutters and repairs to the curtain walls and one of the towers.

HERALDIC SHIELDS AND MEDIEVAL
STONE FIGURES STILL STAND GUARD
ON THE OCTAGONAL TOWERS

DESCRIPTION OF ALNWICK CASTLE 1586

A later survey provides additional domestic details. The inner bailey contained a small garden, a horse mill (necessary in times of siege), a chantry and school served by a friar and, on the south wall, a set of garderobes, or lavatories, which emptied into the Bowburn stream.

The castle then had its prison at the base of the north octagonal tower where there still survives a dungeon or oubliette, into which prisoners could be lowered and kept in confinement. Other underground chambers beneath the Middle Gatehouse and the south guerite (shown in Tresswell's plan) in the outer bailey took inmates when prisoner numbers were heavy.

Subsequently, when the castle was for a time in royal hands, it was written off in defensive terms: it was 'not liable to abide the force of any shot or to hold out any time if it should be assaulted'. Thereafter it developed its importance as the administrative centre of a great barony and the extensive Percy estates. Control of the castle lay in the hands of its constable. The earl's chief officers, his receivers and auditors, came twice a year to collect rents and fines using the Auditor's Tower and the exchequer house at Alnwick Castle. The rent days' takings filled saddlebags which were carried on packhorses, under armed escort, to the earl's counting house in London.

AN ARTIST'S IMPRESSION OF HOTSPUR FOR THE ROYAL SHAKESPEARE COMPANY, 1946

ESPERANCE EN DIEV

Isometric plan of Alnwick
Castle, watercolour
by F.R. Wilson, 1855

An Artist's impression of
Henry, Hotspur's father, First
Earl of Northumberland

WILLIAM THE
LION MONUMENT

RIGHT: MILITARY ARTEFACTS ARE ON
DISPLAY IN THE PERCY TENANTRY
VOLUNTEERS EXHIBITION IN THE
CONSTABLE'S TOWER.

ALNWICK CASTLE
in HISTORY

In 1093 Malcolm Canmore, King of the Scots, son of Duncan and defeater of Macbeth, was killed just north of the castle across the River Aln. In 1174 another Scottish king, William the Lion, was captured just to the west of the castle. These events of the early Norman period are connected with the claims of the Scottish kings to territories of the pre-Conquest earldom of Northumbria. Both kings were making sorties to test the feudal opposition. In 1773 the First Duchess set up a monument to Malcolm from whom she claimed descent. A memorial at the gatehouse to Hulne Park records William's capture.

In the medieval period Alnwick was the chief object of numerous Scottish raids, one of the most disruptive being that of 1448. A decade or more later, when Alnwick became a focus of dispute in the conflict between opposing parties in the War of the Roses, the castle was besieged and changed hands no fewer than five times in the years 1462 to 1464. In 1462, when under siege by Yorkist forces, the castle was manned by a contingent of French gunners who made their escape through the Postern Tower to join a relieving Lancastrian force. Before they fled they poured their

LADY ELIZABETH SEYMOUR WHO
BECAME FIRST DUCHESS PAINTED BY
ALLAN RAMSAY C.1740

cannonballs down the castle well. Some of these, recovered in the course of the 18th century castle restoration, are now on display in the dungeon. The castle landed up in 1464 in Yorkist hands and the Fourth Earl, who joined the Yorkist cause, brought some prosperity back to town and barony after the ravages of civil strife.

The last successful assault made by Scottish raids took place in 1577 when the attackers found entry in the bailey and cleared the castle dungeon and cellars of its prisoners, including the earl's auditors held for suspected fraud. The Civil War (1642–1650) brought problems to Alnwick. The Cromwellian soldiers burned down the township of Walkergate just outside the castle walls. Troopers were billeted in the castle and the surrounding

districts. Complaints were made about the commandeering of horses, fodder and food supplies. Rents were difficult to gather and transport to London which meant a period of uncertain income for the earl.

In September 1650, after the Battle of Dunbar, 6000 Scottish prisoners were lodged for one night 'betwixt the middle and upper gate' of Alnwick castle on their way south to Durham.

Lodging at the castle of a totally different kind took place in the Second World War. Girls from Newcastle Church High School were evacuated to the castle and shared the facilities of the local Duchess's High School for Girls. From 1945, former servants' quarters provided accommodation, first for an emergency teachers training college, then, from 1949–1977, Alnwick College of Education. From 1981 to the present day this part of the castle has been used by American students of St. Cloud State University, Minnesota.

MALCOLM'S CROSS

Castle
RESTORATIONS

During the 17th century and the first half of the 18th century the castle was in decay and the landed estate provided income but no amenity. Parts of the castle were even being leased to local town craftsmen. Canaletto's romantic view of the castle, 1752, barely masks the forlorn state of the fabric.

Division of Percy lands in 1750 meant that the estates in Yorkshire, Cumberland and Sussex were separated from those in Northumberland. The inheritors of these northern lands concentrated their attention on Alnwick. This castle became the absorbing passion of the heiress

Elizabeth Seymour, descendant of the Percys, who together with her husband Hugh, first Earl (1750) then Duke of Northumberland (1766), set about turning a derelict castle into their principal country seat. The castle could offer so little in the way of comfort on their first visit in 1750 that the couple had to stay in the old exchequer house!

CANALETTO WAS ALSO COMMISSIONED TO PAINT SYON HOUSE (BELOW) IN 1749 AND NORTHUMBERLAND HOUSE, LONDON (ABOVE LEFT) IN 1752

Hugh Smithson and Elizabeth Seymour the
First Duke and Duchess of Northumberland

In 1749 a series of famous architects including Daniel Garrett, James Paine and Robert Adam were connected with the transformation of the derelict castle at Alnwick into a palace in the *gothick* style. Parts of the keep were taken down to their foundations and rebuilt. A series of large *gothick* windows at principal level surmounted by smaller ogee windows in the storey above were a distinguishing architectural feature.

PHOTOGRAPH OF THE CASTLE TAKEN JUST PRIOR TO SALVIN'S ALTERATIONS OF THE 1850S

In the outer bailey the south-east tower was transformed into a water tower and close by a new yard with stables and coach houses created. The castle library and chapel occupied the principal level of a new building which linked the middle gatehouse to the keep. In the inner bailey the old eastern tower was replaced. This new tower housed the records of the estate on its lower level and, at its upper level, Robert Adam created a banqueting room which overlooked the newly-planted landscape to the north and east of the castle. Along the wall head to the west of this Record Tower a bower called 'Hotspur's Seat' was erected on the site of an old *guerite*. In front of the keep to the north a terrace was built, creating a vantage point from which to view parkland improvements. Where the medieval garderobes had once stood a gateway was built leading to the newly-created gardens.

'A SOUTH VIEW OF THE TWO OCTAGON TOWERS, POSTERN TOWER (OR SALLY-PORT) AND THE CONSTABLE'S TOWER' – A WATERCOLOUR *C.* 1770

The interior of the keep was completely transformed. In medieval times the quarters for gentle living had been over the gatehouse of the keep. The great hall was the focus of castle living. At the hall's west end were external steps leading down to the courtyard and the castle kitchens.

18th century restoration completely changed the use of space within the keep. The great hall was retained as the new state dining room but westward from it a suite of state rooms was provided, approached from the courtyard by an internal elliptical grand staircase. James Paine was responsible for this restoration work. His successor Robert Adam, who worked for the First Duke at both Northumberland House and Syon, created the new library and chapel in the adjoining middle gateway wing. Continuity in the scheme of architectural work was provided by John Bell of Durham, responsible for many of Alnwick's buildings, who was clerk of works to both Paine and Adam. He resided at the castle during restoration work enjoying the perquisites of the upper servants.

It was John Bell who supervised the 'New Work' of the First Duke. This included restored servant's halls, kitchens, a suite of offices and chambers, brewery, laundry, coach houses and stables, stretching from the new Lion Gateway along the south side of the castle's perimeter wall westwards to the new stable yard.

These ancillary amenities transformed a medieval castle into a modern day palace and in so doing increased almost one hundred-fold the amount of castle building.

Carved figures which decorate the middle gateway and octagonal towers are medieval but those on the other towers and keep are the legacy of the 18th century restoration. The mason James Johnson of Stamfordham is reckoned to

SIR DAVID SMITH'S SKETCH OF A STONE FIGURE WHICH STOOD ON TOP OF THE OLD LION GATEWAY, *C.* 1820

CAST OF COMMEMORATIVE MEDAL OF 1766 CELEBRATING THE COMPLETION OF ALNWICK CASTLE'S RESTORATION

THE WINDOW RECESS OF
THE SALOON, 1823

have taken 20 years carving these figures which festooned the castle. However, many were removed at the time of the 19th century restoration.

Inside the castle, the restored state rooms had elaborate recesses, highly decorated fireplaces in local Denwick stone or marble and ceilings with fan-vaults or armorial designs. The walls of the chapel were decorated with a pedigree of Percy.

These elaborate *gothick* plasterwork interiors were swept away in the mid-19th century restoration. Structural weakness was one reason for this but desire on the part of the Fourth Duke for complete architectural change was another.

Algernon, Fourth Duke, chose to replace the 18th century *gothick* with more serious architecture and in the architect Anthony Salvin employed the finest Victorian exponent of the castle style. Salvin had worked for the Third Duke, building estate churches, including St. Paul's Church, Alnwick, completed in 1846.

Salvin's design included a new square tower named the Prudhoe Tower in honour of Duke Algernon who had been created Baron Prudhoe in 1816. This was built on the south-west flank of the keep and adorned with a *sejant* or sitting lion holding a Percy armorial banner (above). Duchess Eleanor laid the foundation stone in November 1854.

Other additions included the building of the castle chapel to the south side of the Prudhoe Tower and, inside the courtyard of the keep, a *porte-cochère* (covered entrance) with a guard chamber above it. On the north side of the courtyard of the keep a passage was constructed at first floor level over a *loggia* and corbelling to link the state rooms. Long lancet windows capped with carved lintels became the distinctive exterior feature of the keep.

The Falconer's Tower was built on the north side of the outer bailey. Below it, to the east, the gun terrace was extended. A Guest Hall with gallery and timber roof was built on the south side of the coach yard. To the west of the yard a riding school and stables were erected. This restoration of the castle was spread over the years between 1854 and 1867. Salvin was assisted by the architect Frederick R. Wilson and by William Eden Nesfield, Salvin's nephew and the son of William Andrews Nesfield, the garden designer. George Smith of London, who enjoyed an international reputation, was the principal contractor for the work, using a workforce of nearly 400 men, mainly masons and carpenters. Local joiners and specialist technical and engineering companies assisted.

THE FOURTH DUKE

A workmen's dinner was provided for all who helped in the castle restoration works to celebrate the laying of the foundation stone of the Prudhoe Tower in 1854. On each anniversary thereafter until 1864, a workmen's dinner was held when between 700 and 800 sat down to roasts, pies and puddings and beer, pipes and tobacco. In 1859 the occasion was held in tented pavilions in the outer bailey when the newly installed castle kitchens were put to the test. There were toasts, speeches and songs and the Fourth Duke as always was toasted as 'Algernon the Good', the 'chieftain' and the 'saviour of the town'.

The castle today is essentially Algernon's testimony in stone. A few subsequent changes need to be noted. The Record Tower was taken down and rebuilt (most probably with stone from the old Canongate gasworks in the town) in 1885. A draftsmen's office was built in the area of the coachhouse yard where the castle brewery had once stood and a small record tower was built on the south side of the outer bailey.

ANTHONY SALVIN'S DESIGN FOR THE
PRUDHOE TOWER AND CHAPEL, C. 1850

The PERCYS & ALNWICK

1066 – 1403

William de Percy (d. 1096), founder of this family, came to England with William the Conqueror. He came from the Caen region of the Norman duchy where villages still bear the name 'Perci'. He was in the war band of Hugh of Avranches who became Earl of Chester. William took his share of the Norman division of lands and became settled as a magnate in Yorkshire where he held lands of the king, the Earl of Chester and the Bishop of Durham. William reformed the old Saxon abbey of Whitby, Yorkshire, and joined the Crusade, on which venture he died.

In the mid-12th century the heiress **Agnes Percy (d. 1204)** married Jocelin of Louvain, brother of the wife of the Norman king Henry I. Their figures decorated every Percy pedigree reminding the family of the importance of this marriage alliance.

In the political turmoil of the 13th century the Percys found themselves, like so many other barons, opposed to King John: **Richard Percy (d. 1244)** was one of the twenty five magnates appointed to oversee the provisions of Magna Charta. But in the middle of the 13th century the Percy lord was not persuaded by the baronial party of Simon de Montfort and remained royalist. Loyalty and continued service both in council and under arms later recommended Percy when King Edward I pursued his cause in Scotland.

Henry Percy (1273–1314), the first lord of Alnwick, appeared the ideal servant of Plantagenet kingship: warrior against the Scots, Keeper of the Marches, he was also a member of the King's Council and acted as regent in the king's absence. He was summoned to the king's parliament as baron by writ. Who better then to control the great and strategically

One of the series of title deeds relating to the purchase of Alnwick Castle and Barony by Henry Percy in 1309.

important northern barony of Alnwick than this loyal Percy? This old Vescy barony had come under the control of Antony Bec, the powerful Bishop of Durham, who threatened to absorb it into the palatinate lands which would mean its loss to royal control.

However, Bec was persuaded to sell the barony to Henry Percy and the deal was sealed with royal approval in 1309.

In the 14th century the Percys could do no wrong. **Henry, second lord of Alnwick (1314-1352)**, like his father, spent a lifetime consumed in negotiating with the Scots and guarding the Border. His reward was the consolidation of his Northumberland lands: the barony of Warkworth and the lordships of Rothbury and Newburn were granted to him. He helped defeat the Scots at Neville's Cross (1346). The Percy power base came to shift northwards from Yorkshire to Northumberland. Both Henry and his son and successor were buried at the abbey of Alnwick rather than at one of their endowed Yorkshire abbeys.

Political power continued to increase. **Henry Percy (1368–1408)**, whose father had fought at Crécy, warred in France but became increasingly caught up in politics at home. He became Marshal of England (1376) and was created Earl of Northumberland at the coronation of Richard II (1377).

An image of Henry, the First Earl, from a manuscript in the British Museum

It is believed that the use of the crescent in the Percy badge dates from this time: it had once been the badge of the old Saxon earldom of Northumbria. This advancement came not long after a marriage to a widow and heiress who brought two more great northern baronies, those of Prudhoe and Cockermouth, to the family. This consolidated the primacy of the Percys in the Borders.

Increased power was soon used to try to broker kingship: Richard II was forced to stand down and Henry IV set up in his place. When this king no longer suited, then rebellion was resorted to in an attempt to overthrow him. But defeats at Shrewsbury (1403) and Bramham Moor (1408) brought an end to the Percys' grip on political power.

Most famous of all Percys, **Harry 'Hotspur' (b. 1364 d. 1403)** emerged during this period. He is Alnwick's own hero for he was born here at the castle, in the quarters above the gatehouse of the keep. His nickname, 'Hotspur', sums up his quicksilver temperament, courage and impetuousness. He was raised in the tradition of his ancestors. He battled in the Borders; undertook crusade in the marches of eastern Europe; fought on land and sea against France. He was the hero of the chronicler Froissart who relates the quarrel between Douglas the Scot and Hotspur which led to the midnight battle of Otterburn (1388), an event which showed the deep rooted dynastic rivalries of late medieval society. Hotspur was taken prisoner yet his courage was the stuff of heroes.

FIGURE WITH PERCY HERALDIC EMBLEMS FROM MEDIEVAL WOOD CARVING WRESSEL CASTLE, YORKSHIRE

Hotspur's own squire John Harding was his greatest admirer. Harding wrote a history of England which in its account of the 14th and 15th centuries was a story of the greatness, bravery and service to the crown of the Percys. Harding, writing in the mid-15th century, beseeched the king to take note that the Percys held 'the hearts of the people by North and ever had'. Harding had his old master Hotspur in mind. No wonder Shakespeare was so fascinated by Hotspur! The sub-title of his play '*Henry IV Part I*' was after all the '*Life and Death of Henry surnamed Hotspur*'.

1403–1750

In two hundred years following Hotspur's death at the Battle of Shrewsbury (1403) only two Percy earls died in their beds. Of the others, three were killed in battle, two executed and two murdered.

Hotspur's son, **Henry the Second Earl (1416–1455)**, loyal to Henry V who restored him, was a patron of learning, endowing fellowships at Oxford and establishing a chantry and school at the castle. He also built Bondgate Tower at the southern entrance to the town. He died in battle fighting for the Lancastrian cause as did his son, the **Third Earl (1455–1461)**. **The Fourth Earl (1461–1489)** gained notoriety for his allegiance to the cause of Richard III, his failure to intervene in the Yorkist cause at Bosworth Field and his murder by peasantry for his zealousness in collecting taxes for the first Tudor monarch.

The Fifth Earl (1489–1527) was a great courtier at a time when the Tudor court was absorbed in Renaissance magnificence. He escorted the Princess Margaret, daughter of Henry VII, in great pomp and splendour northwards to her marriage with the Scottish king James IV: in the parks at Alnwick the princess shot a deer. No more detailed account survives of the daily life of a great Tudor lord than is provided by this earl's Household Book. The splendour of his own household came close to that of the king; its expense crippled his estates.

The character of his son **Henry the Sixth Earl (1527–1537)**, is intriguing. This Henry was the victim of the powerful central government of Henry VIII. Against the new men who served the king, the old nobility with their old religious faith stood no chance. Henry's fate is made all the more poignant because of his personal circumstances. He was brought up as a page in the household of Cardinal Wolsey yet it fell his lot to arrest Wolsey for the king; he fell in love with Anne Boleyn and wanted to wed her yet he had to stand aside for the sake of the king. In the end, childless, unhappy and dismayed with his brothers' political entanglements, he put his lands into the hands of a king who had caused him and his family so much grief.

ILLUMINATED INITIAL FROM ANNE BOLEYN'S PERSONAL PRAYER BOOK IN ALNWICK CASTLE LIBRARY

Just when the fortunes of the Percys seemed well and truly sunk, a change of monarch brought about their restoration. The accession of Mary brought the restoration of **Thomas Percy Seventh Earl (1557–1572)** to his earldom and his ancestral lands in 1557. There was optimism that he could weld together all those parts of the old local community in his northern barony which had been destroyed or broken down in the turbulence of the times. The earl was urged to take up residence at Alnwick.

Instead, in Queen Elizabeth's reign, he chose the desperate course of rebellion for the old faith and for Mary Queen of Scots and lost all in the chaotic 'Rebellion of the Northern Earls', as his escapade with the Earl of Westmorland was called. Alnwick witnessed the sad spectacle of the Seventh Earl being brought back a prisoner from Scotland on his journey to trial and execution in York.

Thomas's folly sank the family under a cloud of suspicion for the next half century. Thomas and his brother **Henry**, who in turn became **Eighth Earl (1572–1585)**, were sons of Thomas Percy, a leader in the popular uprising, the Pilgrimage of Grace (1536–1537). Authority was suspicious that Henry espoused the old faith and the cause of the Scottish queen and so he was imprisoned in the Tower of London where he was found dead, most probably murdered.

Little did **Henry the Ninth Earl (1585–1632)** imagine on his succession to his father that imprisonment in the Tower would be his fate too. Henry followed the course of a true Renaissance nobleman. To whatever

interest he turned, he gave his full intellectual attention: military tactics; astronomy and navigation; science, particularly alchemy; surveying and cartography. There is little wonder that this nobleman accumulated one of the greatest libraries of his day; was known as the 'Wizard Earl'; patronised scholars and was a friend of Sir Walter Raleigh, through whom he was able to savour the products of the New World.

But, at the height of his success when his support for James of Scotland as monarch to follow Elizabeth brought him even greater influence and wealth, misfortune struck. Important among the Earl's servants was the constable of Alnwick Castle who had local responsibility for administering the castle and barony, controlling bailiffs and collecting rents. The castle constable was the Ninth Earl's distant cousin, Thomas. Thomas was a useful tool in the earl's affairs, particularly well placed to be his messenger to the Scottish court. But he also abused his office, exploited tenants and pocketed moneys. At Syon, the Earl's Middlesex house, Thomas Percy dined with his master on the evening of the 4th November 1605. The next day the plot to blow up the Houses of Parliament was discovered: Thomas Percy was one of the principal gunpowder plotters and was shot dead making his escape in the Midlands.

Though pleading his innocence, the Earl was arrested and confined to the Tower of London where he spent the next 17 years. He was fined a massive sum of £30,000 which indeed forced the Earl to increase the efficiency of his estates so as to raise money to pay it off. In the Tower he suffered no physical hardship: he chose his diet, modified his apartments to his needs, improved the walks, had his gardening done by his Syon gardener, administered his lands, educated his children and met up again with his great friend Raleigh! The Ninth Earl was the last Percy for four centuries to be born in Northumberland. On his release from the Tower he was confined to his Sussex estate.

SIR WALTER RALEIGH'S NAME ON A LIST OF GUESTS OF THE NINTH EARL, WITH POTATOES ON THE MENU, 1591

THE SIGNATURE OF THOMAS PERCY – ONE OF THE MAIN COLLABORATORS IN THE GUNPOWDER PLOT, 1605

THOMAS PERCY SEVENTH EARL (1557–1572)

His son **Algernon Tenth Earl (1632–1668)** only visited Alnwick, as he did in 1640, when matters of state brought him to the North. This Earl learned the lesson of his father's predicament and in the turbulent times of the Civil War steered a very judicious course. He held high office under Charles I being Lord High Admiral and President of the Council of War but held back from full commitment to the royalist cause and so lost his commands. He supported a compromise between king and people which established his reputation for impartiality. After the king was arrested and imprisoned he was made Governor of the Royal Children, who lived at the Earl's house at Syon.

Remarkably the Earl brought his vast lands, including Alnwick, through the Civil War still intact. Algernon was a great patron of artists but his collection of silver and many of his fine old master paintings had to be sold to bear the costs of the times. After this, family involvement with Alnwick declined.

The Eleventh Earl (1668–1670) died young while on The Grand Tour and his only child, the heiress Elizabeth, had to fight off the claims of others to her lands and titles. Her marriage to Charles Seymour, Sixth Duke of Somerset, in 1682 brought control of the estates to a man whose interest lay in court, collecting and horse racing. So

long as his estates provided for his interests he was not much troubled. It was only when his son Algernon Seymour reigned briefly as the **Seventh Duke of Somerset (1748–1750)**, that interest in Percy ancestry was once more rekindled.

ELIZABETH PERCY, SIXTH DUCHESS OF SOMERSET, (b.1667 d.1722) BY HENRI GASCARS

1750 – Present

Enthusiasm for Percy ancestry very quickly and readily rubbed off onto Algernon Seymour's daughter, the heiress **Elizabeth Seymour**. It was she who brought her family back to Alnwick when this portion of the Percy inheritance came to her.

Fascinated by her Northern origins and her 'braw rough ancestors' as she called them, she was overwhelmed by the *gothick* atmosphere of the north. For her, Alnwick was a place to enjoy. She breathed new life into its ancient customs, admired its scenery, entertained its worthies and attended its theatre. Her husband, the Yorkshire man **Hugh Smithson**, **Earl (1750-1766)** and **First Duke**

of Northumberland (1766–1786), boosted the local economy and secured influence and patronage by restoring the castle and parkland.

(center, above:)
ALGERNON TENTH EARL BY SIR ANTHONY VAN DYCK

He modernised the local agriculture and industries, including coalmining and glass-making on the Tyne. Elizabeth and her Duke were encouraged by their chaplain Thomas Percy who provided the Duchess with the details of her pedigree and the history of her ancestors. Such was the impact that Elizabeth Percy had on Alnwick and its environs that, after her death in 1776, her Duke erected monuments to her memory on the estate, including a tower at Brizlee, an observatory at Ratcheugh and a garden house at Hulne Priory.

Elizabeth's son, **Hugh Second Duke (1786–1817)** inherited her enthusiasm for the north. He was the first Percy in centuries to overwinter at Alnwick and set a pattern of management on his estates the influence of which can still be felt. As a lad of 16 he raised a company of recruits from Alnwick to serve in the army with him in the Seven Years War (1756–1763). He became a general in the War of American Independence (1775–1783) and there learned lessons of tactics which he put to good use when he raised his own local volunteers in the Napoleonic conflict. The Fifth Regiment of Foot took the title 'Northumberland Fusiliers' in recognition of his compassion for his men when he was its colonel in Ireland and America. His farming tenants, too, recognised his help and concern when they erected the Tenantry Column at Alnwick in 1816 to celebrate his reign.

Hugh Third Duke (1817–1847) consolidated his father's work and expanded the estates. With his Duchess, Charlotte Florentia, he served both country and local community. He was royal representative in both France and Ireland and his Duchess was Governess to Princess Victoria.

No Percy has benefited the castle, estate and local community more than **Algernon Fourth Duke (1847–1865)** who restored the castle. He was already a man of mature judgement and independent outlook when he succeeded his brother the Third Duke. He had served as midshipman and naval officer in the Napoleonic Wars, after which he became immersed in travel and archaeological exploration. He was one of the first Englishmen to journey to Upper Egypt to record Pharoanic remains there. He was a particularly enlightened landowner who provided well for his dependants in the countryside while also making his possessions an amenity for the wider community to enjoy. In 1851 he sent his own estate workmen to see the Great Exhibition and opened Northumberland House and Syon House to the public. He enjoyed the company of enlightened, open-minded men who shared his enthusiasm for art, architecture and archaeology. His reign was a celebration of independent thought and taste mixed with great compassion: no wonder he was known as Algernon 'the Good'!

George Fifth Duke (1865–1867), Algernon's cousin and grandson of the First Duke's younger son, succeeded in 1865 at the great age of 87. His son **Algernon Sixth Duke (1867–1899)**, who married Louisa,

heiress of Henry Drummond, banker, political philosopher and religious reformer, was a prominent member of the Catholic Apostolic movement which flourished in the high church atmosphere of Victorian England. Both he

and **Henry Seventh Duke (1899–1918)** were active politicians and courtiers who benefited the local community of Alnwick through their establishment of a workingmen's club and bath houses. The Seventh Duke was a keen local historian who undertook excavation of the castle's barbican ditch.

Alan Ian Eighth Duke (1918–1930) was a career soldier who served in South Africa, the Sudan and throughout the First World War. His Duchess, Helen, who served Queen Elizabeth for many years as her Mistress of the Robes, guided the family through the 1930s and the Second World War in which **George Ninth Duke (1930–1940)** was killed.

The long reign of **Hugh Tenth Duke (1940–1988)** provided the Percy family and estates with great stability in a period of post-war uncertainty and latterly modern-day prosperity. He transformed his estates to meet changing requirements of the second half of the 20th century. It was Duke Hugh and his Duchess Elizabeth, who decided to make Alnwick Castle their permanent home and the estates their main interest. The Duke was recognised as a foremost agriculturist of his day. His deep interest in science led him to chair the government investigation into bovine foot and mouth disease (1968) and also the Medical Research Council. In 1950 he opened Alnwick Castle to the general public.

Henry Eleventh Duke (1988–1995) had a passion for film-making and for the history of his ancestor Hotspur. His brother **Ralph Twelfth Duke (1995)**, who has succeeded him, has concentrated his interests on Alnwick and his northern estates. He is married to Jane Richard and they have four children.

The HOUSEHOLD

Some glimpse of the Percy household is possible from as early as the time young John Harding entered Hotspur's service as a page in 1390. The Household Book of the Fifth Earl in the early 16th century reveals the way a great nobleman and his household lived: food supplies, diet, transport, daily prayers and the hierarchy of servants are all listed.

The household was then continually on the move. Later the earls employed a staff of officers responsible for different aspects of their living: steward of the household, purse bearer, foreign paymaster, clerk of the kitchen, cofferer, gentleman of horse, gentleman usher, disburser for apparel. When the Ninth Earl visited Flanders in 1588, he was accompanied by no fewer than 13 liveried servants.

HOUSEHOLD STAFF IN ATTENDANCE AT ALNWICK CASTLE IN 1908, AT THE TIME OF THE ROYAL VISIT

Lavishness of style persisted into the 18th century. When the First Duchess made her summer stay at Alnwick in 1768 she had a staff of 52 including 11 liveried footmen and 3 liveried stablemen. When the family was absent, the castle household was in the charge of a female housekeeper who was allowed to keep gratuities left by castle visitors. Even when permanent castle staff were on board wages the laundry maids still got their pitcher of ale on washdays!

MRS RENWICK, HOUSEKEEPER, BY OSWALD BIRLEY, 1948

Servants moved around with their masters and came with the dukes to reside at Alnwick in summer. Their mode of travel depended on their station. Some came in advance by coach to prepare, some came with the family by coach and others by the accompanying wagon. A usual way was by ship from London to Alnmouth. The Third Duke sometimes sailed north in his yacht.

HUGH THIRD DUKE OF NORTHUMBERLAND AS PORTRAYED BY RICHARD DIGHTON IN 1832

When resident at the castle, servants abided by house rules which regulated their tasks, their times of work, what and where they ate, when they went to bed. The gate porter kept an eye on male servants who were lodged together in the gatehouse. There was a distinct divide between the upper servants, who included the steward, the clerk of the kitchen, the groom of the chambers, the valet de chambre and the butler, and the rest of the household. But the duke regarded all servants as belonging to his 'family', for each of whom he held himself responsible.

The mid-19th century restoration of the castle had a deep impact on the household. Quarters for stable staff were built at first floor level in the coach yard. House staff were quartered to the south side of the middle gateway where Salvin built a spectacular kitchen with a hydraulic lift capable of raising a ton of coal to fire the roasting spit and ovens. To speed up delivery of food from the kitchen to the State Dining Room, an underground passage was constructed to connect the two. The passage lights at ground level are still visible leading from the area of the middle gateway to the base of the wall of the keep where a pulley wheel indicates the location of the dumb-waiter hoist. The kitchen even employed an engine man!

SERVANTS IN SALVIN'S
GREAT KITCHEN, C. 1865

LIVERIED SERVANTS
AT THE CASTLE
A CENTURY AGO

INSTRUCTIONS GIVING AMOUNTS TO BE SPENT ON
CHRISTMAS PRESENTS BY HOUSEHOLD SERVANTS, 1913

Social stability and growing affluence of later Victorian England caused servant numbers to grow. At the end of the 19th century household staff numbered 86. There were 39 women, with 6 laundry-maids, 6 housemaids, 6 kitchen maids as well as personal and travelling maids. Of the 47 men, 4 were footmen and 16 were coachmen and stablemen. Today, under the Household Controller, there are 8 full-time and 12 part-time members of staff.

STAFF AWAITING GUESTS AT A BANQUET IN
THE GUEST HALL TO CELEBRATE THE COMING
OF AGE OF LORD WARKWORTH, 1892

The INTERIORS

The style of decoration of Alnwick Castle interiors was the brainchild of the Fourth Duke and the invention of the Roman architect and archaeologist Luigi Canina (b. 1795 d. 1856). Canina's professional life had been devoted to restoration work. He met the Duke in Rome in 1853 and discussed the scheme for Alnwick's interior restoration. Prior to this Canina had restored the Villa Borghese, one of the great 16th century Roman palaces, after the ravages of the 1848 revolution in Rome.

Alnwick followed the style of 16th century Roman palaces in its interior decoration. Rome had craftsmen and workshops to provide all decorative skills necessary. Communications by sea and by land were so well developed by mid–19th century that these artefacts in finished form could safely be conveyed all the way from Rome to Alnwick. Distinguished Italian artists and craftsmen were persuaded to participate in the Duke's scheme.

In the end, the Duke decided to create a school of wood carving at Alnwick. Anton Leon Bulletti, a brilliant young Florentine carver, was engaged to come to Alnwick to teach the school. This breathed a new purpose into the restoration work since the object of the school was to provide English carvers with the skills and accomplishments of their continental counterparts.

*BRITANNIA BY
GIUSEPPE NUCCI*

The carvers' workshops, provided with skylights, were situated in the coach yard. The carving school which was composed of 21 carvers (drawn principally from Glasgow and Newcastle) and 6 apprentices, operated from 1854 to 1863. The development of carving skills led to the adoption of a saying in the town that Alnwick was to decorative arts what Cremona was to the violin!

SECTION OF CARVED FRIEZE IN THE DINING ROOM

Luigi Canina came to Alnwick in 1856 to survey and discuss progress of work with the Duke and British architects who approved the scheme. He was accompanied by his right-hand man Giovanni Montiroli (b. 1817 d. 1888) who was an accomplished draftsman. After Canina's death Montiroli supervised the work both in Rome and at Alnwick. In Rome craftsmen produced the marble fireplaces and balustrades in best Carrara marble. In the workshop of Giovanni Taccalozzi models of the fireplaces made in gesso were first sent to England for the Duke's approval. Italian sculptors of repute carved the statuary figures.

DRAWING ROOM DETAILS

ABOVE LEFT: CARVED WOOD WINDOW SHUTTER
LEFT: MONTIROLI'S CEILING DESIGN, 1856
RIGHT: CARVED MASK OF THE MEDUSA ON
DOOR BOSS

The COLLECTIONS

Throughout the generations members of the family have shown enthusiasm for collecting. The Ninth Earl's patronage of scholars led him to amass books which form the basis of the castle library today. Algernon the Tenth Earl followed the example of his royal master, King Charles I, and became a collector of old masters as well as a patron of the great artists of his day, particularly Van Dyck and Lely.

Charles Sixth Duke of Somerset was a lover of house sales and liked nothing better than to send his house steward to hunt for bargains: the William Dobson paintings are part of his legacy. His granddaughter Elizabeth Seymour, in her turn, enjoyed winning a bargain in the saleroom or with a dealer. Her tastes were widespread and she collected practically anything. Travelling in the Low Countries, she journeyed in her own chaise with her servants in an accompanying coach and a wagon at the rear in which to load her acquisitions as she moved from dealer to dealer! Her husband was regarded as the exemplar of good taste: Chippendale's book of furniture designs, the *Director* (1754), was dedicated to him and in his patronage were included Robert Adam the architect, Canaletto the artist, Joseph Wilton the sculptor and John Linnell the cabinet maker.

DETAIL OF MARQUETRY, FRENCH
COMMODE C. 1690

TRIPLE PORTRAIT FOLLOWER OF TITIAN. THE PORTRAIT IS
ALLUDED TO IN BYRON'S POEM *BEPPO*, 1817

The Third and Fourth Dukes used their great wealth to expand the collections of their ancestors. The Third Duke followed the fashion of the Prince Regent in his patronage of the furniture makers Morel and Hughes and the eminent dealers of the day such as Robert Fogg.

He patronised British sculptors in Rome, particularly the northern sculptor John Graham Lough. He completed the great silver-gilt dinner service begun by his grandfather. Algernon, Fourth Duke, mixed convention with ideals in his collecting. His purchase of an important gallery of paintings in Rome in 1854, 'the Camuccini Collection', was the last and possibly the greatest purchase made at one go by an individual Englishman abroad. This gallery of 74 paintings included work by Bellini, Raphael, Guido Reni, Andrea del Sarto, Badalocchio and Claude. The collection derives its name from the two brothers Pietro and Vincenzo Camuccini who formed the gallery in Rome during the latter part of the18th and beginning of the 19th century. The interiors of Alnwick in the Roman *cinquecento* style created an ideal setting for them. The Duke also collected Venetian paintings of the Renaissance.

Three principal family residences have closed: Northumberland House in London was demolished by government order to allow road development (1874) and Stanwick Hall, Yorkshire (1922) and Albury House, Surrey (1965) were sold. Important pictures and furniture from these houses are now located at Alnwick Castle.

RIGHT: ONE OF A PAIR OF EBONY CABINETS MOUNTED WITH *PIETRA
DURA* PANELS SUPPLIED BY DOMENICO CUCCI IN 1683 FOR LOUIS
XIV'S PALACE OF VERSAILLES.

CAVALRY FLINTLOCK PISTOL OF 1802,
BY MORTIMER OF LONDON

A POWDER HORN OF THE
PERCY TENANTRY VOLUNTEERS

The GUARD CHAMBERS

Equipment of the Percy Tenantry Volunteers (1798–1814) - pistols, powder flasks and horns, swords and sergeants' pikes - masks the sombreness of this entrance. An exhibition about these volunteers is displayed in the Constable's Tower.

LOWER GUARD CHAMBER

17TH CENTURY BRONZE VENETIAN DOOR
KNOCKER DEPICTING NEPTUNE STANDING
BETWEEN A SEA-HORSE AND A SEA-UNICORN

AN ARRANGEMENT OF CAVALRY SWORDS
AND POWDER HORNS OF THE PERCY
TENANTRY VOLUNTEERS

VIEW OF THE GRAND STAIRCASE

SCULPTURE OF LOUISA, SIXTH DUCHESS, BY PIERS CONNOLLY

The statue of the seated figure of Louisa, Sixth Duchess was sculpted by the North American Piers Connolly, 1869–1871. The figure of *Action* is by Joseph Gott, a British sculptor who worked in Rome and was patronised by the Third Duke.

VIEW FROM THE TOP OF THE GRAND STAIRCASE

UPPER GUARD CHAMBER

The Upper Guard Chamber was one of the last works to be undertaken in the 19th-century restoration. The Italian architects introduced a style for this vestibule which harmonised with the rest of the interiors.

Giovanni Montiroli designed the marble mosaic floor in the Venetian style and it was laid in the summer of 1864 by the Roman craftsman Luigi Malfatti. The marble balustrade and candelabra flanking the staircase were made in Roman workshops and Giuseppe Nucci, the chief figurative sculptor, carved the figures of Britannia and Justice which stand in alcoves in the east wall.

The ceilings of the Guard Chamber and the staircase are in stucco, the work of William Brien, master plasterer. The arches and groins of the staircase, the panel mouldings and the pier arches dividing the chamber from the staircase carry foliate designs which continue into the mouldings of the Guard Chamber ceiling. The Percy coat of arms decorates the central octagonal coffer.

The four canvas frieze panels high on the Guard Chamber walls represent scenes from the old border ballad 'Chevy Chase' which tells of a legendary skirmish between Percy and Douglas in the Borders in which both chiefs die. The ballad was edited and published by the First Duke's chaplain Thomas Percy in his *Ancient Reliques of English Poetry* (1765).

'Chevy Chase' is also a Northumbrian pipe-tune. It became the signature tune of the Percy dukes and was played by an ensemble of pipes in the Guard Chamber when welcoming guests to social functions. Paintings in the Guard Chamber include the full length portrait of the Tenth Earl as Lord High Admiral by Van Dyck. Below the portrait is the Earl's admiral's baton. The painting is flanked by four Canalettos: two London scenes on the theme of the rebuilding of Westminster Bridge, one of Syon House painted in 1749 and one of Windsor Castle from Percy Lodge, the country seat of the Seventh Duke of Somerset.

Opposite hang paintings of the Sixth Duke and Duchess of Somerset by Sir Godfrey Kneller. Below is a pair of landscapes by Orizonte, favourite pictures of the First Duke which had hung at Stanwick Park, his Yorkshire home. Philip de Laszlo's portrait of Helen, Eighth Duchess of Northumberland, was painted in 1916.

Paintings from the Camuccini Collection, purchased by the Fourth Duke in 1854, include Claude's *Sunset*, Lorenzo Lotto's *Infancy Crowning Death*, and Domenico Feti's *Blind Leading the Blind*. Furniture includes two pairs of mid-18th century pier tables and armchairs by the master carver and cabinet maker John Linnell.

The ANTE-LIBRARY

The Ante-Library is the first room which shows off the craftsmanship of the Alnwick school of carving. Ornamentation carved in pine and gilded was fixed by pins, screws and brackets to the coffered ceiling. The dado is inlaid with sycamore. Four views of Rome by Italian artists, intended to draw attention to the importance of that city to the castle's decorative scheme, were commissioned for this room but they were never hung here.

Instead, paintings of the Venetian school were hung. The *Lady with a Lute* by Palma Vecchio, the *Triple Portrait* attributed to Titian and the *Artist and his Pupils* by Bernardino Licinio were purchased by the Fourth Duke from the Manfrini Gallery, Venice.

The fresco of *The Visitation* by Sebastiano del Piombo, described by Giorgio Vasari, was purchased by the Duke from the collector Rev. W. Davenport-Bromley in 1853. Titian's *Bishop and his Secretary* was part of the Tenth Earl's collection of Old Masters, which came to him from the collection of the Duke of Buckingham, favourite of Charles I. Of the two which hang alongside it, one, *Ecce Homo*, is by Titian, and the other is attributed to that artist.

Originally the Ante-Library was hung in green Milanese silk. The present wall hangings, dating from 1970, are by Colefax and Fowler.

LEFT: PALMA VECCHIO'S *LADY WITH A LUTE*
HANGS ON THE WEST WALL OF THE ANTE-LIBRARY

THE VISITATION
PART OF A FRESCO BY
SEBASTIANO DEL PIOMBO

ECCE HOMO
BY TITIAN

*THE BISHOP OF ARMAGNAC
AND HIS SECRETARY
GUILLAUME PHILANDRIER*
BY TITIAN

The LIBRARY

*The Library room occupies the principal floor of Salvin's Prudhoe Tower. The bookshelves,
in light oak inlaid with sycamore, were installed by George Smith and the coffered ceiling
(like all others throughout the state rooms) by the local cabinet maker Thomas Robertson.
Giovanni Montiroli designed three trophies with art, music and science as their subjects.
The fourth is dedicated to archaeology and the navy, the two main interests of the Fourth Duke.*

Marble busts of Francis Bacon, William Shakespeare and Isaac Newton decorate the three fireplaces.

John Martin, librarian of the Inner Temple, was employed by the Duke to build up his library collection. Extensive purchases at the dispersal sales of collectors and scholars of repute expanded an already distinguished collection. The Ninth Earl (b. 1564 d. 1632) had assembled one of the finest personal Renaissance libraries in England to help fellow scholars and as a solace during his many years of confinement in the Tower of London. His son Algernon (b. 1602 d. 1668), who was educated at the Tower, inherited his passion for books. The First Duchess's maternal ancestors, particularly her 'blue stocking' mother Frances Thynne (d. 1754) brought numerous choice items to the collection.

As a patron of the lifeboat movement, the Fourth Duke saw fit to equip his library as a coastal weather station complete with barometer and weather gauges. Daily weather records were maintained and the information passed to national weather records.

Oak library furniture was made by Thomas Robertson, the local cabinetmaker.

IN THE BACKGROUND IS THE BUST OF SIR ISAAC NEWTON BY GIOVANNI STRAZZA *C.* 1860

WILLIAM
SHAKESPEARE
BY FRANCESCO
FABI-ALTINI *C.* 1860

GIOVANNI MONTIROLI'S
PEN AND WASH STUDIES
FOR THE LIBRARY
CEILING'S TROPHIES

BOOKS OF THE NINTH EARL
OF NORTHUMBERLAND

The two paintings in the library recess are *Bacchus and Ariadne* attributed to Nicolas Poussin, and a portrait of the present Duke and Duchess by Nicky Philipps. In the original scheme of decoration, marble reliefs by McDonald of the Fourth Duke and Duchess decorated the tops of the recess bookshelves. The chandelier, supplied by William Collins in 1822, originally hung in the Great Dining Room of Northumberland House.

GILTWOOD ARMCHAIR, PART OF A LARGE SET SUPPLIED BY MOREL AND HUGHES FOR NORTHUMBERLAND HOUSE IN 1823

The SALOON

The influence of Italian design is exhibited to the fullest extent in the ceilings, fireplaces, doors, window shutters and friezes of the Saloon and Drawing Room. Before the decision was made to create a school of carving, it had been envisaged that only Roman craftsmen would be used. Alessandro Mantovani, one of the important artists then engaged in the decoration of the Vatican palace, was recommended by the influential Cardinal Antonelli, an art connoisseur, to undertake works for the Duke. Mantovani was asked to produce estimates for designs for painted doors, metal window shutters and dados as well as friezes. In the end carved woodwork was preferred.

BOULLE CABINET DETAIL

The Saloon was the first room to be completely restored. The Saloon and the Drawing Room are complementary. Each has two pairs of double doors with foliate decoration in walnut and carved central bosses: lion heads for the Saloon and Medusa heads for the Drawing Room. Each has a fireplace carved in Taccalozzi's workshop with figurative work by Nucci: Dacian slaves in the Saloon, caryatides in the Drawing Room. Each room is decorated with a frieze painted by Mantovani.

THE FIREPLACE CARVED IN 1857 BY GIOVANNI TACCALOZZI IN ROME WITH DACIAN SLAVES BY GIUSEPPE NUCCI

PORTRAITS BY SIR PETER LELY OF JOSCELINE PERCY, ELEVENTH EARL OF NORTHUMBERLAND (b. 1644 d. 1670),
AND HIS WIFE LADY ELIZABETH WRIOTHESLEY (d. 1690)

New silk for the walls of the Saloon and Drawing Room has been woven copying the original designs of the hangings ordered from Ambrosio Osnago in Milan in 1864. The two pairs of Boulle cabinets were made in Paris for the Saloon under commission from John Webb in 1854. The pair of premier and contre-partie Boulle tables either side of the fireplace date from the early 19th century. Paintings in the Saloon include portraits of the Eleventh Earl and his wife, Elizabeth Wriothesley, by Peter Lely and their daughter Elizabeth, the Percy heiress by Henri Gascars. Portraits of the Tenth Earl and Queen Henrietta Maria are by Van Dyck. Also on the fireplace wall hang two paintings by William Dobson (b. 1610 d. 1646), recognised as the most important English painter before Hogarth. At each end of the room hang a pair of Canalettos: two Venetian scenes and views of Alnwick Castle and Northumberland House. Other paintings were part of the Camuccini collection.

PORTRAIT OF THE ARTIST WITH NICHOLAS LANIER AND SIR CHARLES COTTERELL BY WILLIAM DOBSON, C. 1642

The DRAWING ROOM

This is the most sumptuous room in the Italian style and the one which fully
demonstrates the skills of the decorative designer Giovanni Montiroli in successfully creating a
symmetrical design for such an awkwardly-shaped ceiling.

Alessandro Mantovani painted the frieze of the Drawing Room (and that of the Saloon) in oil on canvas. The frieze was mounted on frames so as to fit the shape of the room. Mantovani spent July and August 1856 at Alnwick supervising this work and working on the background colours of the ceiling. The frieze bears the design of putti, medallions and classical heads in the style used by Guilio Romano for the 16th-century decoration of the Castel Sant'Angelo, Rome, which was an inspiration for the Italian architects in their designs for Alnwick. Carving a pair of lime-wood window shutters occupied one whole year of a craftsman's work-time. Montiroli designed the frames for the overmantel mirrors in the Drawing Room and Saloon which were carved by the Alnwick school.

TWO DETAILS OF THE MARQUETRY TABLE C. 1865 DEPICTING THE FIVE SENSES

The pair of *pietra-dura* cabinets bear the cypher of Louis XIV and were made at the French king's Gobelins factory for his palace at Versailles in 1683. They are the work of the Florentine craftsman Domenico Cucci. They were purchased by the Third Duke in 1822 from Robert Fogg, a London dealer who supplied furniture to George IV.

TWO OF THE IVORY CARVINGS, BOUGHT BY THE FIRST DUCHESS ON HER CONTINENTAL TRAVELS

The ebonised cabinet was made by Morel and Hughes in 1823 for this same Duke and was designed to house the collection of ivories bought by the First Duchess on her travels abroad in the 1760s and 1770s.

Paintings of the Camuccini collection include Andrea del Sarto's *Portrait of a Young Man*, Guido Reni's *The Crucifixion* and Sisto Badalocchio's *Tancred and Clorinda and Rinaldo and Armida*. The distinctive picture frames of the Alnwick school of carving surround the Sisto Badalocchios. There is also J.M.W. Turner's *View of the Temple of Jupiter Panhellenios*, 1816 (right) acquired by the Fourth Duke, a friend of C.R. Cockerell, the architect, who had excavated the temple site in 1811 and advised the Duke on Alnwick's restoration. On the wall opposite hangs Keirincx's *Orpheus and the Thracian Women*, which the First Duchess records in her journal (*c.* 1770) as being purchased by her in the Low Countries for £12.1s.6d!

VIEW OF THE TEMPLE OF JUPITER PANHELLENIOS, 1816, BY J.M.W TURNER

The DINING ROOM

The Great Hall had been at the centre of castle life in medieval times. Rearrangements of rooms
in the 18th century did not lessen its importance. It had daily use by the family when resident:
the alcove was used for breakfasting. It was here also that the First Duke and Duchess entertained
local gentry and worthies on their open days. On such occasions the Duchess had her piper play to the
guests from beneath the dining room windows in the inner bailey.

Mantovani's scheme for a painted frieze for this room
was not accepted so its decoration fell to the school of
carving whose panels of garlanded heraldic motifs and
intervening stylized cornucopias of fruits created the
school's masterpiece. The ceiling, carved in Brunswick
pine, left ungilded, is decorated with the heraldry of Percy.
It replaced an 18th century heraldic ceiling in plaster.

The room was lit by two candelabra wound down
through trap doors in the ceiling, either side of the
central coffer, to hang above the dining table. The great
fireplace, exhibited in Italy by Taccalozzi before it was
sent to Alnwick, takes up the heraldic theme in its frieze
celebrating the Fourth Duke and his Duchess in the
badges of Percy and Grosvenor.

AN ARMORIAL DESIGN BY MONTIROLI FOR THE CEILING

LOUISA HARCOURT BY WILLIAM OWEN, C. 1810

The Buffets and side tables were made locally in the workshops of the cabinet maker Thomas Robertson. The seat furniture includes a set of dining chairs and a set of side chairs with two armchairs which in the 18th century had been at the First Duke's family seat of Stanwick Hall. The table silver includes the plateau make by Edward Thomason in 1818 to a design by the Third Duchess and the silver-gilt candelabra and cups form part of the service created by the London silversmiths, Rundell, Bridge and Rundell 1822-1830.

Over the fireplace hang portraits of the First Duke and Duchess in a frame by the Alnwick school. On the southern wall hangs the portrait of the Fourth Duke in admiral's uniform by Sir Francis Grant. To the right, above the door, hangs the portrait of Louisa Harcourt by William Owen. Louisa romantically and clandestinely married the young Lord Lovaine in 1801. She died in 1848 but he lived on to succeed his cousin to the ducal title in 1865 at the age of 87. This duke's portrait by Gustav Pope hangs on the north wall. From this marriage alliance the present Percy line descends.

CORNER SECTION OF CARVED FRIEZE

The
BREAKFAST ROOM

This room was untouched by the mid-19th century restoration but by the 1890s the late
Gothic hammer roof was falling to pieces. Eustace Balfour, the architect, restored the room in
Queen Anne style for the Sixth Duke. The flat stucco ceiling is decorated with the heraldic design
of the crescent and the fetterlock. The wall covering is heavily embossed paper which imitates leather.
The fireplace surround is of fossilised marble; within it is an ancient armorial grate.

The 18th century painted canvas, which hangs above the gallery, is part of a set by the French artist Clermont once used to decorate the marquees at Syon House when the First Duchess held her fêtes.

The pair of paintings either side of the fireplace are attributed to Peter Hartover who worked in the years 1674–1690. They depict the castles of Alnwick (pictured below) and Warkworth. The Alnwick painting provides the most detailed illustration of the castle before its 18th century restoration; it also provides a south view of the town showing such landmarks as Bondgate Tower, the Tollbooth and Alnwick Abbey outside the town.

This room is now used for temporary exhibitions.

Alnwick Castle

The CHINA GALLERY

This corridor was originally designed by Salvin to provide service access to the State Rooms. In 2006 the gallery, formerly hung with pictures, was completely re-displayed. The current layout shows off the Northumberland Collection's Meissen, Chelsea and Paris porcelain in a manner that was inspired by the interior design of the European porcelain palaces of the 17th and 18th centuries.

There are two Meissen services. One, a dinner service decorated with fantastic animals, foliage and insects, dates from *circa* 1745, some of the earliest pieces of hard paste porcelain made in Europe. The other service, is of a later date, *circa* 1780, and is decorated with scenes from Aesop's Fables.

The Paris dessert service, from the Dagoty factory, dates from the 1820s, each piece painted with an individual topographical scene of France, or well-known tourist spot in Italy and Switzerland. This grand service was probably bought by the 3rd Duke in 1825 when he was in Paris in attendance at the coronation of King Charles X as the personal representative of King George IV.

DETAIL OF A HAND-PAINTED PLATTER FROM THE GREAT MEISSEN DINNER SERVICE, DEPICTING A RHINOCEROS

TUREEN FROM MEISSEN DINNER SERVICE C. 1745 AND PLATE FROM LATER MEISSEN DINNER SERVICE ILLUSTRATED WITH AESOP'S FABLES, C. 1780

The CHAPEL

This room is a mid-19th century addition to the keep by the architect Anthony Salvin *and combines English Victorian gothic with Italian art in its internal decoration. In the Middle Ages the Percy household was abustle with the activities of priests and clerics; taking divine service, praying for the souls of past Percy lords, taking care of the muniments and libraries and keeping the household accounts. The household could not have functioned without its men of the cloth. Throughout the many Percy baronies, patronage and material support were offered to monasteries, secular clergy, hermits, chantry priests, scholars and teachers.*

Here at Alnwick canons and friars of two religious houses within the parklands received Percy support, so did a considerable chantry established in what is now the parish church. In addition, a chantry served by three priests was established at the castle in the middle of the 14th century to pray for Percy souls and to run a school. Its chapel was built in the inner bailey close to the Constable's Tower. The ruined and stripped gable ends of this chapel survived into the 18th century and are shown in Canaletto's painting of the castle.

The remains of this medieval chapel were swept away in the restoration work of the First Duke and Duchess. Robert Adam completed the restoration of the castle in the early 1780s with the building of a library room and chapel on the principal level of the new castle wing which stretched from the keep to the Middle Gateway. The chapel occupied the southern part of this building, above the gateway itself. Adam decorated the walls of the chapel with the Percy family tree and placed within it a sarcophagus as a memorial to the First Duchess. He also designed a lectern and priest's chair, now on display here, recognised as among his finest furniture in the late *gothick* style.

This furniture is all that remains of Adam's chapel which disappeared in the restoration of the mid–19th century. While the old library and chapel were transformed into a principal suite of rooms for the Fourth Duke and Duchess, the architect Anthony Salvin was left in something of a quandary concerning the siting of a new chapel.

ROBERT ADAM'S *GOTHICK* CHAIR, ON DISPLAY IN THE CHAPEL

Anthony Salvin produced one design of a freestanding chapel close to the Middle Gateway in the inner bailey; and another of a freestanding chapel sited in the outer bailey. In the end, economy and convenience won the day, and the chapel was incorporated in the fabric of the restored keep on its south side.

The chapel's gothic ceiling and lancet windows are in keeping with Salvin's design for the ground floor of the castle; its mosaic marble walls are of Italian design and manufacture and complement the Italian style so pronounced in the castle's principal rooms. It is only here in the chapel that both styles are brought together. The decoration of the stone bosses of the roof groins are the work of the eminent sculptor James Forsyth of London.

Salvin's chapel offered a daily opportunity for family members and household staff, to come together for a common act of worship. The ducal party entered the gallery of the chapel on the principal level directly from the state rooms. Below the gallery, at ground level, the servants assembled in their pews from the different servants' halls. Household rules obliged all servants whose duties allowed to attend prayers at 8am.

358

MR DUTENS TUTOR TO LORD ALGERNON PERCY

LOUIS DUTENS (b. 1730 d. 1812), RECTOR OF ELSDON, NORTHUMBERLAND; TUTOR TO ALGERNON, YOUNGER SON OF THE FIRST DUKE AND DUCHESS, DURING HIS GRAND TOUR 1768–1771

In the Sixth Duke's time (1867–1899) the form of the service was set out in a published book of family prayers.

It was the duty of the duke's chaplain to lead family prayers. The chaplain usually had other responsibilities, such as ministry of the local church or the duties of duke's secretary or tutor to his children. Services regularly took place in the chapel until the 1970s including family marriage and baptism.

Part of the Fourth Duke's haul of treasures from his travels in Italy and on the Continent in the 1860s included the French tapestries which now cover the Chapel walls. He placed them in the suite of rooms which Salvin restored for him at Warkworth Castle. It was not until the 1960s that they were hung in the chapel at Alnwick Castle. Two of the tapestries, made in Paris *circa* 1625, show scenes from the life of Constantine the Great, the first Christian emperor: one his baptism, the other his vision. The five mid-18th century Aubusson tapestries tell the biblical story of the blind Tobit and his dutiful son Tobias who finds the cure for his father's blindness.

LEFT: *THE NATIVITY* BY GIOVANNI LANFRANCO C. 1605

THOMAS PERCY (b. 1729 d. 1811), ANTIQUARIAN, POET, SCHOLAR; CHAPLAIN TO THE FIRST DUKE AND DUCHESS OF NORTHUMBERLAND, LATER BISHOP OF DROMORE

'FORGING POWER'

Postern Tower
The Dukes and their
MUSEUM

'RECORDING OF
EGYPTIAN INSCRIPTIONS'

The Castle Museum, opened to the public in 1826, played a full part in the Fourth Duke's scheme of restoration. It was his intention to promote the serious study of the archaeology of the North and he surrounded himself with the keenest and best informed minds for that purpose. Under his patronage important investigations and digs were undertaken; the number of artefacts increased through his own enthusiastic collecting and purchasing; and the process of cataloguing the collection was begun. Archaeological digs continue to take place on estate lands today, adding new finds to the collection.

FRESCO PAINTING
FROM POMPEII

THE POSTERN TOWER

THE RUDGE CUP

TOMBSTONE OF
LORETA DE BOTRY

A TRANSLATION OF
THE INSCRIPTION
READS: '*LORETA
DE BOTRY
OVERTHROWN BY
CRUEL DEATH LIES
IN THIS GRAVE, MAY
SHE LIVE AND HAVE
A CROWN OF JOY*'

ROMAN DRINKING VESSEL

THE WITHAM
SWORD

SHIELD FROM THE BATTLE
OF SHREWSBURY, 1403

MEDIEVAL ANDIRON

Constable's Tower
Percy Tenantry Volunteers
EXHIBITION

No single act in Percy history demonstrates better the workings of a great landed estate, the interplay of characters and events and the fusing of national and local concerns, than the raising of these military volunteers at the time of danger of Napoleonic invasion. Models of members of the force shown here are based on real-life persons whose records survive among the papers of the Percy Tenantry Volunteers (1798-1814).

THE CONSTABLE'S TOWER

EARL PERCY (LATER THIRD DUKE) IN THE COMMANDING OFFICER'S UNIFORM OF THE PERCY TENANTRY VOLUNTEERS. DETAIL OF THE PORTRAIT BY THOMAS PHILLIPS

THE PERCY TENANTRY VOLUNTEERS
Raised 1798

CORPORAL THOMAS CALL

CORPORAL JOHN STRONG

CAPTAIN MARSHALL

SGT. MAJOR JOSEPH BROWN

The equipment and accoutrements of the force are displayed in the lower gallery of the Constable's Tower, the lower guard chamber of the castle and on the Terrace.

The COACH HOUSE

Here is displayed the state coach complete in Percy livery. In origin this was a royal coach and carried the royal livery when it transported the Third Duke as King George IV's personal representative to the coronation of Charles X in France in 1825.

The coach now carries the arms of the Seventh Duke and Duchess, re-painted in 1902 for their use at the coronation of King Edward VII.

More recently, the coach was used at the weddings of the Twelfth Duke's daughters, Lady Catherine and Lady Melissa Percy in 2011 and then 2013.

Livery of the coachmen and footmen are in the Percy colours of blue and gold. In the Second Duke's time (1786-1817) liveried servants first wore their new annual issue of uniform on the Sovereign's birthday. For the journey from London to Alnwick the footmen accompanying the coach were armed. At the beginning of the 20th century the coachman was replaced by a chauffeur for the Duke's motorcar.

THE STATE COACH WAS LAST USED IN JULY 2013 FOR THE WEDDING OF LADY MELISSA PERCY, YOUNGEST DAUGHTER OF THE DUKE OF NORTHUMBERLAND.

The
ALNWICK GARDEN

Writers throughout history have extolled *the virtues of the garden. Its enjoyment is one of the chief benefits of the country house.*

When, in the mid-18th century, Elizabeth Seymour and her husband decided to make Alnwick their principal country seat, gardens and pleasure grounds became a necessity. Gardens were created on the south side of the castle. In order to provide adequate garden area, one of the town's roads had to be diverted, and the ground at the backs of many of the town houses bought up. A garden gateway then had to be put through the castle walls in the inner bailey. At first the walled enclosure was simply called the 'kitchen garden' and was really a nursery for young trees with espalier fruit trees round the walls and soft fruits in the border. The surrounding pleasure grounds developed so as to merge with the newly-planned landscape which was adjacent.

Alnwick gardens and pleasure grounds then underwent a century of development. Hothouses were built for raising pineapples, the coal to fire boilers being produced locally at the duke's coal mine at Shilbottle. In 1811 the gardener's cottage was built. The head gardener had the charge of 20 others under him.

Produce from the hothouses was sent down to the duke's table in London by the mail coach. Pineapples from Alnwick were sent to Paris for the Third Duke when he was special ambassador there in 1825 and to Dublin when he was Lord Lieutenant 1829-1830. This Duke, who was a plant collector, brought plants and seeds from all over the world to be reared at Alnwick. He built a large conservatory in the gardens which were opened to the public one day a week. For her part the Third Duchess transformed Alnwick into a garden of flowers. The garden area was continually expanded. The gardens were at their

most complete in the middle years of the
19th century when the Fourth Duke
called upon William Andrews Nesfield to
design the main garden for him. Nesfield
was eminent among Victorian gardeners,
being the first to apply the term 'garden
architecture' to his work. He first visited
Alnwick in 1848 and submitted a final set

INSIDE THE OLD
CONSERVATORY C. 1870

of garden
plans to
the Duke
by 1860. His
scheme provided
Alnwick with an
Italianate garden.

At the end of the 19th century
the gardens were at their grandest with yew
hedges in topiary, a double avenue of limes, acres
of flower garden, five grapehouses, five pinehouses
and a conservatory. The First World War brought an end to gardening on this scale. The
gardens rallied to help 'dig for victory' during the Second World War but in the 1950s the
glasshouses were dismantled and the garden site turned over to a forestry nursery.

Today In the new millennium, Jane, Twelfth Duchess of Northumberland, is creating imaginative
and innovative gardens within the walls of the former old garden. Some of the best garden
designers in Britain and Europe have brought together a scheme to create water features and
lighting displays by the aid of new technology within gardens dominated by topiary design. This
offers an experience in garden architecture unlike anything else in England.

The new development is designed as a garden for all seasons to be open twelve months a year.
Incorporated within The Alnwick Garden is a pavilion to provide facilities for refreshments and
functions, a visitor centre and shops and one of the largest tree-houses in the world. The Garden is
run as a registered charity, with all proceeds being used to maintain and administer the gardens to
ensure their future development.

The first phase of this ambitious project was officially
opened by HRH The Prince of Wales in September 2002,
and the second phase in September 2007.

HRH THE PRINCE OF WALES AND THE DUCHESS
OF NORTHUMBERLAND AT THE OPENING OF THE
SECOND PHASE OF THE ALNWICK GARDEN

DETAIL FROM J.M.W. TURNER'S PAINTING THE
TEMPLE OF JUPITER PANHELLENIOS, AEGINA

VIEW OF THE BRIDGE SPANNING THE RIVER ALN
ON THE NORTHERN SIDE OF THE CASTLE. BUILT
C. 1770, IT IS ADORNED WITH A PERCY LION

'A DISTANT VIEW OF
HULNE ABBEY'.
W. BEILBY. OCT. 20TH 1773

Alnwick
HULNE PARK

'A VIEW IN HULNE PARK
BELOW THE ABBEY'.
W. BEILBY. OCT. 20TH 1773

*In medieval times there were three parks which flanked the castle on its north, west and south.
Of these Hulne Park survives today. The parks fulfilled the purpose of providing the lordship with
timber on which the castle depended for its maintenance. The old saying was 'destroy the forest,
pull down the castle'. Keeping deer for hunting was its second main purpose.*

ALNWICK
CASTLE →

ALNWICK ABBEY

THE
GATEHOUSE
ALNWICK
ABBEY

ROBERT NORTON'S MAP WHICH SHOWS THE PARKS AT
ALNWICK (COLOURED GREEN) IN 1624

PARK FARM

STONE
FIGURES
AT HULNE
PRIORY
C. 1776

Emparking of Hulne took place in the 13th century. In 1224 King Henry III made a gift of 5 bucks and 10 does to stock Alnwick parks which were under the care of the park keepers, foresters, wallers and pallisers. Hulne Park extended over 4,500 acres within a walled enclosure stretching some thirteen miles. At the end of the middle ages the park held nearly 1000 fallow deer and some 1800 oak trees grew within it. In 1488 the Fourth Earl built a tower at the priory of Hulne to serve as a hunting lodge.

The early Vescy lords founded two religious houses within their parklands. Alnwick Abbey, which was one of the most important northern religious houses, was established near the River Aln in 1147. The impressive gatehouse of the abbey still stands in the south-east corner of the park north of the river. In the midst of Hulne Park a friary was begun in 1265, one of the earliest English Carmelite foundations. Friars were allowed to gather honey in the forest; wild bees still make their home at Hulne.

Hulne Park was transformed in the 18th century. The First Duke decided to landscape the park and increase the planting of trees, particularly beech and pine. With the aid of his own gardener Thomas Call and the famous landscape designer Lancelot 'Capability' Brown, the Duke created a park landscape which embraced not only the confines of Hulne but also the pasture lands to the north and east of the castle. Other improvements included the building of the Lion Bridge by Adam and the Denwick Bridge by Robert Mylne. The site of Hulne priory became the chief feature to be visited on a coach drive in the park. Brizlee Tower, designed by Robert Adam and built in 1781 by the First Duke as a memorial to his Duchess, dominates the park's skyline; its inscription records the achievement of the Duke in the planting of trees and the creating of the park.

In the 1820s Park Farm, with its farm buildings and farmhouse by John Green, became the Duke's home farm. A variety of deer and exotic Indian cattle were a feature of the park at this time. The stone-walled compounds in which they were kept still survive along the main drive in the park. The main Forest Lodge with its entrance gateway at the west end of Ratten Row was built in 1859 to a design by Anthony Salvin.

Today Hulne Park still fulfils two chief purposes of its medieval past. It is still a place of sport being the headquarters of the Duke's keeper since 1763. The park also continues as one of the main locations for estate forestry. The sawmills there have been working since 1874 and continue to supply timber for the estate. In the early 1830s the size of the park was reduced by a third. All the land within the park's perimeter is farmed in-hand.

A VIEW OF HULNE PRIORY FROM BRIZLEE TOWER

HULNE PRIORY

BRIZLEE TOWER

LOOKING NORTH EAST, ALONG THE
PERIMETER WALL, BETWEEN THE POSTERN
TOWER AND THE CONSTABLE'S TOWER

The LANDED ESTATE

A HEMMEL, TRADITIONAL
NORTHUMBERLAND FARM BUILDING

In recent times the size and conformation of the Northumberland estates have changed. Some lands have been sold off, others bought. The most notable change was the take-over of the North Tyne estate at Kielder by the Forestry Commission in 1932 to form the largest man-made forest in Europe.

Administering the estates is the job of the agent and his staff who occupy the buildings on the south side of the outer bailey between the Clock Tower and the Auditor's Tower. The interior of this wing was left undisturbed by the 19th century restoration and is the work of the architect John Bell and the joiner Vincent Shepherd.

VIEW OF ALNWICK FROM BRIZLEE, BY THOMAS GIRTIN, C. 1800

VIEW FROM HOTSPUR'S SEAT, LOOKING NORTH
ACROSS THE MEADOWS OF THE RIVER ALN

Percy lands today retain their overwhelmingly agricultural character as they have done over the centuries. The estates include 115 tenanted farms and 400 cottages. Many of the farms are tenanted by families whose association with the estate goes back over generations. The estate forester, whose office is medieval in origin has the charge of some 6000 acres of woodlands, planted to make use of otherwise marginal land. The sporting character of the estate is maintained on its rivers and moorlands. In today's world, the estate provides a buttress for a distinctive country way of life built on values drawn from closeness to and understanding of the countryside and enthusiasm for maintaining an environment which can be enjoyed by all. The Duke and his estates seek to be at the centre of this process.

ALNWICK CASTLE FROM THE RIVER ALN

WILLIAM de PERCY, m. Emma de Port
(d. 1096)

ALAN de PERCY, m. Emma, dau. of Gilbert de Gant
(d. c. 1135)

WILLIAM de PERCY, m. Alice de Tonbridge
(d. c. 1175)

AGNES de PERCY, m. Jocelin of Louvain
(d. c. 1204)

HENRY de PERCY, m. Isabel, dau. of   Richard de PERCY,
(d. c. 1198)   Adam de Brus   (d. c. 1244)

WILLIAM de PERCY, m. Ellen, dau. of Ingram de Balliol
(d. c. 1245)   (d. c. 1281)

HENRY de PERCY, m. Eleanor, dau. of John de Warenne,
(b. c. 1235 d. 1272)   Earl of Surrey (d. c. 1282)

HENRY de PERCY, m. Eleanor, sister of Sir Richard de
(b. c. 1273 d. 1314)   Arundel (d. 1328)

HENRY de PERCY, m. Idonia, dau. of Robert de Clifford
(d. 1352)   (d. 1365)

HENRY de PERCY, m. Mary, dau. of Henry, Earl
(d. 1368)   of Lancaster (d. 1362)

HENRY de PERCY, m. Margaret, dau. of Ralph de Nevill,
(b. 1341 d. 1408) cr.   Lord Nevill of Raby (d. 1372)
Earl of Northumberland
1377; attainted 1406

Sir HENRY PERCY, m. Elizabeth, dau. of Edmund
better known as 'Hotspur'   Mortimer, Earl of March (d. 1417)
(b. 1364 d. 1403)

HENRY de PERCY, m. Eleanor, dau. of Ralph Nevill,
(b. 1393 d. 1455) cr. Earl   Earl of Westmorland
of Northumberland 1416

HENRY PERCY, m. Eleanor,
(b. 1421 d. 1461)   dau. of Richard de Poynings
Earl of Northumberland,   (d. 1484)
attainted 1461

HENRY PERCY, m. Maud, dau. of William Herbert,
restored as 4th Earl of   Earl of Pembroke (d. c. 1485)
Northumberland,
(b. c. 1449 d. 1489)

HENRY ALGERNON PERCY, m. Catherine,
5th Earl of Northumberland,   dau. of Sir Robert Spencer,
(b. c. 1478 d. 1527)   (d. 1542)

HENRY   m. Mary, dau. of   Sir Thomas   m. Eleanor,
PERCY,   George Talbot,   Percy   sister
6th Earl of   4th Earl of   (executed   of George
Northumberland   Shrewsbury   at Tyburn   Harbottle
(b. c. 1502 d. 1537)   (d. 1572)   1537)   of Beamish

THOMAS   m. Anne, dau. of   HENRY PERCY   m. Catherine,
PERCY,   Henry Somerset,   8th Earl of   dau. of John
7th Earl of   2nd Earl of   Northumberland   Nevill,
Northumberland   Worcester   (b. c. 1532 d. 1585)   Lord Latimer
(b. c. 1528 d. 1572)   (d. 1591)   (d. 1596)

HENRY PERCY, K.G. m. Dorothy, dau. of Walter
9th Earl of Northumberland,   Devereux, 1st Earl of Essex
(b. 1564 d. 1632) imprisoned   (d. 1619)
in the Tower 1605-1622)

ALGERNON PERCY, K.G. m. Elizabeth, dau. of
10th Earl of Northumberland,   Theophilus Howard, 2nd
(b. 1607 d. 1668)   Earl of Suffolk (d. 1705)

JOSCELINE PERCY m. Elizabeth, dau. of Thomas
11th Earl of Northumberland,   Wriothesley, 4th Earl of
(b. 1644 d. 1670)   Southampton (1690)

ELIZABETH PERCY m. (l) Earl of Ogle (2) Thomas Thynne
(b. 1667 d. 1722)   (3) Charles Seymour, 6th Duke of Somerset

ALGERNON SEYMOUR Earl of Hertford, m. Frances, dau.
(b. 1684 d. 1750), Succeeded as 7th Duke of Somerset   of Hon. Henry
1748; created Earl of Northumberland 1749 with   Thynne
remainder in default of male heirs to his son-in-law   (d. 1754)

ELIZABETH   m. Sir Hugh Smithson, K.G. (b. 1714/15 d. 1786) Succeeded
SEYMOUR   as Earl of Northumberland 1750 taking name and arms of
(b. 1716 d. 1776)   Percy; created 1st Duke of Northumberland 1766

HUGH   m. Frances Julia, dau.   Algernon Percy   m. Isabella, dau. of
PERCY, K.G.   of Peter Burrell of   1st Earl of   Peter Burrell
2nd Duke,   Beckenham, Kent   Beverley   of Beckenham,
(b. 1742 d. 1817)   (b. 1752 d. 1820)   (b. 1750 d. 1830)   Kent (d. 1812)

HUGH   m. Charlotte   ALGERNON   m. Eleanor, dau. of
PERCY, K.G.   Florentia, dau.   PERCY, K.G.   Richard Grosvenor,
3rd Duke of   of Edward Clive,   4th Duke of   2nd Marquess of
Northumberland   Earl of Powis   Northumberland   Westminster
(b. 1785 d. 1847)   (b. 1787 d.1866)   (b. 1792 d. 1865)   (b. 1820 d.1911)

GEORGE PERCY m. Louisa, dau. of Hon. James Archibald
5th Duke (b. 1778 d. 1867)   Stuart-Wortley Mackenzie (b. 1781 d.1848)

ALGERNON GEORGE PERCY, m. Louisa, dau. of Henry Drummond of
K.G. 6th Duke (b. 1810 d. 1899)   Albury Park, Surrey (b. 1813 d.1890)

HENRY GEORGE PERCY, K.G. m. Edith. dau. of George Douglas
7th Duke (b. 1846 d. 1918)   Campbell, 7th Duke of Argyll
(b. 1849 d. 1913)

ALAN IAN PERCY, K.G. m. Helen, dau. of Charles Gordon-Lennox,
8th Duke (b. 1880 d. 1930)   7th Duke of Richmond (b. 1886 d. 1965)

HENRY GEORGE   HUGH ALGERNON m. Elizabeth, dau. of 8th
ALAN PERCY   PERCY, K.G. 10th   Duke of Buccleuch
9th Duke (b. 1912 d.1940)   Duke (b. 1914 d. 1988)   (b. 1922)

HENRY ALAN WALTER   RALPH GEORGE   m. Jane, dau. of
RICHARD PERCY   ALGERNON PERCY   John Richard
11th Duke (b. 1953 d. 1995)   12th Duke (b. 1956)   (b. 1958)

Compiled from *The Complete Peerage* edit, by H.A. Doubleday and Lord Howard de Walden

Filming at ALNWICK CASTLE

Alnwick Castle and Hulne Park are amongst the most filmed locations in the north and have played host to many film and television productions over the years. These include **Becket** with Peter O'Toole and Richard Burton; **Mary Queen of Scots** with Vanessa Redgrave; **Ivanhoe** with Anthony Andrews and Sam Neill; **Robin Hood – Prince of Thieves** with Kevin Costner; the award-winning production of Elizabeth with Cate Blanchett and Joseph Fiennes; and most recently **Harry Potter and the Philosopher's Stone** and **Harry Potter and The Chamber of Secrets**.

A SCENE FROM THE FAMOUS HARRY POTTER AND THE PHILOSOPHER'S STONE

SCENES IN *ELIZABETH*: CARNAGE ON THE BANKS OF THE RIVER ALN (ABOVE); AND THE TRANSFORMED INNER BAILEY (RIGHT)

Television has used the facilities for a diverse range of productions, such as *The Antiques Roadshow, Flog It, Robin of Sherwood, Blackadder, The Fast Show,* several episodes of the *Catherine Cookson* series, and *Tales from Northumberland* with Robson Green.

HULNE ABBEY DRESSED AS MAID MARION'S HOUSE FOR THE HOLLYWOOD FEATURE *ROBIN HOOD – PRINCE OF THIEVES,* STARRING KEVIN COSTNER

THE INNER COURTYARD PLAYS HOST TO YOUNG ARTHUR WITHDRAWING EXCALIBUR FROM THE STONE; A SCENE FROM *THE DARK KNIGHT*